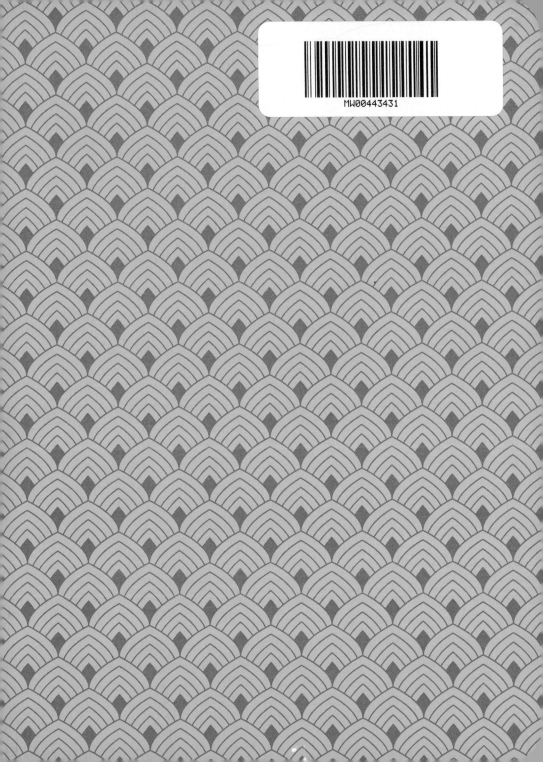

SOBER
JOURNAL

PETER PAUPER PRESS, INC.
WHITE PLAINS, NEW YORK

PETER PAUPER PRESS
Fine Books and Gifts Since 1928

OUR COMPANY

In 1928, at the age of twenty-two, Peter Beilenson began printing books on a small press in the basement of his parents' home in Larchmont, New York. Peter—and later, his wife, Edna—sought to create fine books that sold at "prices even a pauper could afford."

Today, still family owned and operated, Peter Pauper Press continues to honor our founders' legacy—and our customers' expectations—of beauty, quality, and value.

Written and compiled by Ian Thrasher and Barbara Paulding

Designed by David Cole Wheeler
Image used under license from Shutterstock.com

Copyright © 2019
Peter Pauper Press, Inc.
202 Mamaroneck Avenue
White Plains, NY 10601 USA
ISBN 978-1-4413-2882-3
Printed in China
7 6 5 4 3 2

Visit us at www.peterpauper.com

CONTENTS

A NEW DAY: JOURNALING RECOVERY

This prompted, interactive journal is a tool on your road to recovery.

As you write in these pages, one day at a time, you chart the course of intention and resolve, with its gifts and challenges.

Summarize your story in the opening pages, *My Journey to Here*.

In the chart that follows, *The Sober List*, record your intentions and insights, triggers and strategies.

Journal your journey, one day and one page at a time, in the *Daily Pages*. Write about any wins or difficulties of the day. Each page features an inspirational quote.

In the final section, *The Road Ahead*, reflect on the journey so far, and use the insight of clear vision to chart your course in the days ahead.

Persistence is critical.
Being creative and persistent is even better.

—KATIE COURIC

My Journey to Here

What is your story? Write the narrative that brings you to this point in your life.

The Sober List

Create your own personal reference list of goals and motivations (below), and temptations with accompanying techniques for handling them (right page). All of these are subject to change over time.

INTENTIONS AND INSIGHTS

TRIGGERS AND STRATEGIES

DAILY PAGES

In this main section, journal a page a day.

What was significant? Were there any gifts or challenges? What did you feel grateful for? What was difficult?

Each page features a quote—words of wisdom to inspire or encourage—and a "sober today" checkbox.

DATE: _____ ☐ Sober today

Today's story:

_____

_____

_____

_____

_____

_____

_____

_____

Gifts and challenges:

_____

_____

_____

Courage doesn't always roar. Sometimes courage is the quiet voice
at the end of the day saying, "I will try again tomorrow."
—MARY ANNE RADMACHER

11

DATE: _____   ☐ Sober today

Today's story:

_____

_____

_____

_____

_____

_____

_____

_____

Gifts and challenges:

_____

_____

_____

_____

I am an old man and have known a great many troubles,
most of which never happened.
—MARK TWAIN

DATE: _____   ☐ Sober today

Today's story:

_____

_____

_____

_____

_____

_____

_____

Gifts and challenges:

_____

_____

_____

_____

We have the power to choose, moment by moment,
who and how we want to be in the world.

—JILL BOLTE TAYLOR

DATE: _____

☐ Sober today

Today's story:

_____

_____

_____

_____

_____

_____

_____

_____

Gifts and challenges:

_____

_____

_____

Yesterday is not ours to recover,
but tomorrow is ours to win or to lose.

—LYNDON B. JOHNSON

DATE: _____   ☐ **Sober today**

Today's story:

_____

_____

_____

_____

_____

_____

_____

_____

Gifts and challenges:

_____

_____

_____

_____

Finish each day and be done with it.
You have done what you could.

—RALPH WALDO EMERSON

DATE: _____   ☐ **Sober today**

Today's story:

_____

_____

_____

_____

_____

_____

_____

_____

_____

_____

Gifts and challenges:

_____

_____

_____

_____

So keep moving forward. And don't be frustrated when your path gets messy because it will get messy. You'll fall and you'll fail along the way. Wildly. Embrace the mess. ... Get ready for it. And don't let the potential to fail stop you from moving forward.

—OCTAVIA SPENCER

DATE: _____   ☐ Sober today

Today's story:

_____

_____

_____

_____

_____

_____

_____

_____

Gifts and challenges:

_____

_____

_____

_____

There is nothing either good or bad, but thinking makes it so.
—WILLIAM SHAKESPEARE

DATE: _____ ☐ Sober today

Today's story:

_____

_____

_____

_____

_____

_____

_____

_____

Gifts and challenges:

_____

_____

_____

_____

Resistance is the first step to change.
—LOUISE HAY

DATE: _____   ☐ Sober today

Today's story:

_____

_____

_____

_____

_____

_____

_____

_____

Gifts and challenges:

_____

_____

_____

*What you do makes a difference, and you have to decide
what kind of difference you want to make.*

—JANE GOODALL

DATE: _____   ☐ Sober today

Today's story:

_____

_____

_____

_____

_____

_____

_____

_____

_____

Gifts and challenges:

_____

_____

_____

_____

*Think for yourself, and let others enjoy
the privilege of doing so too.*

—VOLTAIRE

DATE: _____ ☐ **Sober today**

Today's story:

_____
_____
_____
_____
_____
_____
_____
_____
_____

Gifts and challenges:

_____
_____
_____
_____

You have to have emptiness before it can be filled.
You have to exhale before you can inhale.
—TOM YEOMANS

DATE: _____   ☐ Sober today

Today's story:

_____

_____

_____

_____

_____

_____

_____

_____

_____

Gifts and challenges:

_____

_____

_____

_____

Our very lives depend only on truth.
—BILL HICKS

DATE: _____ □ Sober today

Today's story:

_____
_____
_____
_____
_____
_____
_____
_____
_____

Gifts and challenges:

_____
_____
_____
_____

*I am the bended, but not broken. I am the power of the
thunderstorm. I am the beauty in the beast. I am the strength
in weakness. I am the confidence in the midst of doubt.*

—KIERRA C. T. BANKS

DATE: _____ ☐ **Sober today**

Today's story:

_____

_____

_____

_____

_____

_____

_____

_____

_____

Gifts and challenges:

_____

_____

_____

_____

The love that you withhold is the pain that you carry.
—ALEX COLLIER

DATE: _____   ☐ Sober today

Today's story:

_____

_____

_____

_____

_____

_____

_____

Gifts and challenges:

_____

_____

_____

The curious paradox is that once I accept myself
just as I am, then I can change.
—CARL ROGERS

DATE: _____   ☐ Sober today

Today's story:

_____

_____

_____

_____

_____

_____

_____

_____

Gifts and challenges:

_____

_____

_____

_____

I am not a has-been. I am a will-be.
—LAUREN BACALL

DATE: _____ ☐ Sober today

Today's story:

_____

_____

_____

_____

_____

_____

_____

_____

Gifts and challenges:

_____

_____

_____

You have to believe in yourself when no one else does—
that makes you a winner right there.
—VENUS WILLIAMS

DATE: _____ ☐ **Sober today**

Today's story:

_____

_____

_____

_____

_____

_____

_____

_____

Gifts and challenges:

_____

_____

_____

_____

Half the game of getting ahead is getting started.
—AUTHOR UNKNOWN

DATE: _____

Today's story:

_____

_____

_____

_____

_____

_____

_____

Gifts and challenges:

_____

_____

_____

_____

*Everybody is a genius. But if you judge a fish by its ability to climb a tree,
it will spend its entire life believing it's stupid.*

—AUTHOR UNKNOWN

DATE: _____

Today's story:

_____

_____

_____

_____

_____

_____

_____

_____

_____

Gifts and challenges:

_____

_____

_____

_____

*The tests we face in life's journey are not to reveal our
weaknesses but to help us discover our inner strengths.*

—KEMI SOGUNLE

DATE: _____   ☐ **Sober today**

Today's story:

_____

_____

_____

_____

_____

_____

_____

_____

_____

Gifts and challenges:

_____

_____

_____

_____

*Don't demand that things happen as you wish, but wish that
they happen as they do happen, and you will go on well.*
—EPICTETUS

DATE: _____   ☐ Sober today

Today's story:

_____

_____

_____

_____

_____

_____

_____

_____

Gifts and challenges:

_____

_____

_____

_____

No matter how bad things are, you can always make things worse.
—RANDY PAUSCH, *THE LAST LECTURE*

DATE: _____   ☐ Sober today

Today's story:

_____

_____

_____

_____

_____

_____

_____

_____

Gifts and challenges:

_____

_____

_____

_____

At the center of your being you have the answer;
you know who you are and you know what you want.

—M. J. RYAN

DATE: _____ ☐ Sober today

Today's story:

_____

_____

_____

_____

_____

_____

_____

_____

_____

_____

Gifts and challenges:

_____

_____

_____

Every day, think as you wake up, today I am fortunate to be alive,
I have a precious human life, I am not going to waste it.

—DALAI LAMA

DATE: _____ ☐ Sober today

Today's story:

_____

_____

_____

_____

_____

_____

_____

_____

Gifts and challenges:

_____

_____

_____

Sometimes you just got to give yourself
what you wish someone else would give you.

—PHILLIP C. MCGRAW

DATE: _____ Sober today

Today's story:

_____

_____

_____

_____

_____

_____

_____

_____

Gifts and challenges:

_____

_____

_____

_____

I took a deep breath and listened to the old brag of my heart.
I am, I am, I am.

—SYLVIA PLATH

DATE: _____

☐ Sober today

Today's story:

_____

_____

_____

_____

_____

_____

_____

_____

Gifts and challenges:

_____

_____

_____

Action precedes motivation.
—ROBERT J. MCKAIN

37

DATE: _____ ☐ Sober today

Today's story:

_____

_____

_____

_____

_____

_____

_____

_____

Gifts and challenges:

_____

_____

_____

_____

You have to participate relentlessly in the manifestation
of your own blessings.
—ELIZABETH GILBERT

DATE: _____ ☐ Sober today

Today's story:

_____

_____

_____

_____

_____

_____

_____

_____

Gifts and challenges:

_____

_____

_____

_____

Our knowledge has made us cynical. Our cleverness, hard and unkind.
We think too much and feel too little. More than machinery,
we need humanity. More than cleverness,
we need kindness and gentleness.
—CHARLIE CHAPLIN

DATE: _____   ☐ **Sober today**

Today's story:

_____

_____

_____

_____

_____

_____

_____

_____

_____

_____

Gifts and challenges:

_____

_____

_____

_____

You can't defeat the darkness by keeping it caged inside of you.
—SETH ADAM SMITH

DATE: _____ ☐ Sober today

Today's story:

_____

_____

_____

_____

_____

_____

_____

_____

_____

Gifts and challenges:

_____

_____

_____

_____

We teach best what we most need to learn.
—RICHARD BACH

DATE: _____ □ Sober today

Today's story:

_____

_____

_____

_____

_____

_____

_____

_____

_____

_____

Gifts and challenges:

_____

_____

_____

*My identity shifted when I got into recovery. That's who I am now,
and it actually gives me greater pleasure to have that identity than to be
a musician or anything else, because it keeps me in a manageable size.*

—ERIC CLAPTON

DATE: _____   ☐ Sober today

Today's story:

_____

_____

_____

_____

_____

_____

_____

_____

Gifts and challenges:

_____

_____

_____

_____

Fiery lust is not diminished by indulging it, but inevitably by leaving it ungratified. As long as you are laying logs on the fire, the fire will burn. When you withhold the wood, the fire dies, and God carries the water.

—RUMI

DATE: _____ ☐ Sober today

Today's story:

_____

_____

_____

_____

_____

_____

_____

_____

_____

Gifts and challenges:

_____

_____

_____

_____

*When everything seems to be going against you, remember that
the airplane takes off against the wind, not with it.*
—HENRY FORD

DATE: _____   ☐ Sober today

Today's story:

_____

_____

_____

_____

_____

_____

_____

_____

Gifts and challenges:

_____

_____

_____

_____

If I only knew who in fact I am, I should cease to behave as what
I think I am; and if I stopped behaving as what
I think I am, I should know who I am.

—ALDOUS HUXLEY, *ISLAND*

DATE: _____   ☐ Sober today

Today's story:

_____

_____

_____

_____

_____

_____

_____

_____

Gifts and challenges:

_____

_____

_____

This discipline and rough treatment are a furnace to extract
the silver from the dross. This testing purifies the gold
by boiling the scum away.

—RUMI

DATE: _____

Today's story:

_____

_____

_____

_____

_____

_____

_____

_____

_____

_____

Gifts and challenges:

_____

_____

_____

_____

*The moment you become aware of the ego in you, it is strictly speaking
no longer the ego, but just the old conditioned thought-pattern.
Ego implies unawareness. Awareness and ego cannot coexist.*

—ECKHART TOLLE

47

DATE: _____ ☐ **Sober today**

Today's story:

_____

_____

_____

_____

_____

_____

_____

_____

_____

Gifts and challenges:

_____

_____

_____

_____

When you awake in the morning, think of what a precious privilege it is
to be alive, to think, to enjoy, to love.

—MARCUS AURELIUS

DATE: _____   ☐ Sober today

Today's story:

_____

_____

_____

_____

_____

_____

_____

_____

Gifts and challenges:

_____

_____

_____

Patience is bitter, but its fruit is sweet.
—JOHN CHARDIN

DATE: _____   ☐ Sober today

Today's story:

_____

_____

_____

_____

_____

_____

_____

_____

_____

Gifts and challenges:

_____

_____

_____

_____

That which we persist in doing becomes easy to do,
not that the nature of the thing has changed,
but our power to do has increased.

—HEBER J. GRANT

DATE: _____   ☐ Sober today

Today's story:

_____

_____

_____

_____

_____

_____

_____

_____

_____

_____

Gifts and challenges:

_____

_____

_____

_____

We are what we pretend to be, so we must be careful
about what we pretend to be.

—KURT VONNEGUT

DATE: _____

Today's story:

_____

_____

_____

_____

_____

_____

_____

_____

_____

_____

Gifts and challenges:

_____

_____

_____

_____

I am the master of my fate,
I am the captain of my soul.
—WILLIAM ERNEST HENLEY, "INVICTUS"

DATE: _____   ☐ Sober today

Today's story:

_____

_____

_____

_____

_____

_____

_____

Gifts and challenges:

_____

_____

_____

_____

As one goes through life, one learns that if you don't paddle
your own canoe, you don't move.
—KATHARINE HEPBURN

DATE: _____   ☐ Sober today

Today's story:

_____

_____

_____

_____

_____

_____

_____

_____

_____

Gifts and challenges:

_____

_____

_____

_____

The overvaluation of money, status, and competition poisons our personal relations. The flourishing life cannot be achieved until we moderate our desires and see how superficial and fleeting they are.

—EPICTETUS

DATE: _____   ☐ Sober today

Today's story:

_____

_____

_____

_____

_____

_____

_____

_____

_____

Gifts and challenges:

_____

_____

_____

_____

*By three methods may we learn wisdom: First, by reflection, which is the
noblest; second, by imitation, which is the easiest; and third,
by experience, which is the bitterest.*

—CONFUCIUS

DATE: _____ ☐ Sober today

Today's story:

_____

_____

_____

_____

_____

_____

_____

_____

_____

_____

_____

_____

Gifts and challenges:

_____

_____

_____

_____

Namaste means that my soul acknowledges yours—not just your light,
your wisdom, your goodness, but also your darkness,
your suffering, your imperfections.

—L. R. KNOST

DATE: _____   ☐ Sober today

Today's story:

_____

_____

_____

_____

_____

_____

_____

_____

Gifts and challenges:

_____

_____

_____

_____

The mark of your ignorance is the depth of your belief in
injustice and tragedy. What the caterpillar calls the end
of the world, the master calls a butterfly.

—RICHARD BACH

DATE: _____ ☐ Sober today

Today's story:

_____

_____

_____

_____

_____

_____

_____

_____

_____

Gifts and challenges:

_____

_____

_____

When two people have come into touch with each other,
without any doubt, they have something in common.
How should a bird fly except with its own kind?
—RUMI

DATE: _____

☐ Sober today

Today's story:

_____

_____

_____

_____

_____

_____

_____

_____

_____

Gifts and challenges:

_____

_____

_____

_____

The shoe that fits one person pinches another;
there is no recipe for living that suits all cases.
—CARL JUNG

DATE: _____ ☐ Sober today

Today's story:

_____

_____

_____

_____

_____

_____

_____

_____

_____

_____

_____

Gifts and challenges:

_____

_____

_____

_____

*Change the way you look at things
and the things you look at change.*
—WAYNE DYER

DATE: _____

☐ **Sober today**

Today's story:

_____

_____

_____

_____

_____

_____

_____

_____

Gifts and challenges:

_____

_____

_____

_____

If you're going through hell, keep going.
—WINSTON CHURCHILL

DATE: _____   ☐ Sober today

Today's story:

_____

_____

_____

_____

_____

_____

_____

_____

Gifts and challenges:

_____

_____

_____

_____

Whatever a man sows, he will reap in return.

—SAINT PAUL

DATE: _____

Today's story:

_____

_____

_____

_____

_____

_____

_____

_____

_____

Gifts and challenges:

_____

_____

_____

_____

> *If you want to reach a state of bliss, then go beyond your ego*
> *and the internal dialogue. Make a decision to relinquish the need*
> *to control, the need to be approved, and the need to judge.*
>
> **—DEEPAK CHOPRA**

DATE: _____ ☐ Sober today

Today's story:

_____

_____

_____

_____

_____

_____

_____

_____

Gifts and challenges:

_____

_____

_____

_____

Let your hopes, not your hurts, shape your future.
—ROBERT H. SCHULLER

DATE: _____ ☐ Sober today

Today's story:

_____

_____

_____

_____

_____

_____

_____

_____

_____

Gifts and challenges:

_____

_____

_____

_____

We must not be enemies. Though passion may have strained,
it must not break our bonds of affection.

—ABRAHAM LINCOLN

DATE: _____   ☐ Sober today

Today's story:

_____

_____

_____

_____

_____

_____

_____

_____

Gifts and challenges:

_____

_____

_____

_____

Truth alone will endure, all the rest will be swept away
before the tide of time.
—MAHATMA GANDHI

DATE: _____

☐ Sober today

Today's story:

_____

_____

_____

_____

_____

_____

_____

_____

Gifts and challenges:

_____

_____

_____

_____

If you don't know where you're going,
any road will take you there.
—GEORGE HARRISON

DATE: _____   ☐ Sober today

Today's story:

_____

_____

_____

_____

_____

_____

_____

_____

Gifts and challenges:

_____

_____

_____

_____

The two most important days of a man's life are
the day on which he was born and the day on which
he discovers why he was born.

—AUTHOR UNKNOWN

DATE: _____   ☐ Sober today

Today's story:

_____

_____

_____

_____

_____

_____

_____

_____

_____

_____

Gifts and challenges:

_____

_____

_____

_____

Sometimes you can only find Heaven by slowly backing away from Hell.
—CARRIE FISHER

DATE: _____   ☐ Sober today

Today's story:

_____

_____

_____

_____

_____

_____

_____

_____

Gifts and challenges:

_____

_____

_____

_____

Effort and courage are not enough
without purpose and direction.
—JOHN F. KENNEDY

DATE: _____   ☐ Sober today

Today's story:

_____

_____

_____

_____

_____

_____

_____

_____

Gifts and challenges:

_____

_____

_____

_____

When you want something, all the universe conspires
in helping you to achieve it.
—PAULO COELHO

DATE: _____   ☐ **Sober today**

Today's story:

_____

_____

_____

_____

_____

_____

_____

_____

_____

_____

Gifts and challenges:

_____

_____

_____

_____

Change will not come if we wait for some other person or if we wait for
some other time. We are the ones we've been waiting for.
—BARACK OBAMA

DATE: _____   ☐ Sober today

Today's story:

_____

_____

_____

_____

_____

_____

_____

_____

Gifts and challenges:

_____

_____

_____

_____

I believe that anyone can conquer fear by doing the things
he fears to do, provided he keeps doing them until he gets
a record of successful experience behind him.
—ELEANOR ROOSEVELT

DATE: _____

Today's story:

_____

_____

_____

_____

_____

_____

_____

_____

_____

Gifts and challenges:

_____

_____

_____

_____

Find out who you are and be that person.
—ELLEN DEGENERES

DATE: _____

Today's story:

_____

_____

_____

_____

_____

_____

_____

Gifts and challenges:

_____

_____

_____

_____

That which can be destroyed by the truth should be.
—P. C. HODGELL

75

DATE: _____ ☐ Sober today

Today's story:

_____

_____

_____

_____

_____

_____

_____

_____

_____

_____

Gifts and challenges:

_____

_____

_____

_____

*We often ask, "What's wrong?" Doing so, we invite painful seeds of sorrow
to come up and manifest. … We would be much happier if we tried to stay
in touch with the healthy, joyful seeds inside of us and around us.
We should learn to ask, "What's not wrong?" and be in touch with that.*

—THICH NHAT HANH

DATE: _____   ☐ Sober today

Today's story:

_____

_____

_____

_____

_____

_____

_____

_____

Gifts and challenges:

_____

_____

_____

_____

The world needs all you can give.

—EDWARD O. WILSON

DATE: _____

Today's story:

_____

_____

_____

_____

_____

_____

_____

_____

_____

Gifts and challenges:

_____

_____

_____

_____

*For the great doesn't happen through impulse alone, and is
a succession of little things that are brought together.*

—VINCENT VAN GOGH

DATE: _____   ☐ **Sober today**

Today's story:

_____

_____

_____

_____

_____

_____

_____

_____

_____

Gifts and challenges:

_____

_____

_____

This one step—choosing a goal and sticking to it—
changes everything.
—SCOTT REED

DATE: _____   ☐ Sober today

Today's story:

_____

_____

_____

_____

_____

_____

_____

_____

_____

_____

Gifts and challenges:

_____

_____

_____

_____

People often say that motivation doesn't last.
Well, neither does bathing—that's why we recommend it daily.

—ZIG ZIGLAR

DATE: _____   ☐ Sober today

Today's story:

_____

_____

_____

_____

_____

_____

_____

_____

_____

Gifts and challenges:

_____

_____

_____

_____

Success demands singleness of purpose.
—VINCE LOMBARDI

DATE: _____   ☐ Sober today

Today's story:

_____

_____

_____

_____

_____

_____

_____

_____

_____

Gifts and challenges:

_____

_____

_____

_____

*Without goals, and plans to reach them, you are like a ship
that has set sail with no destination.*

—FITZHUGH DODSON

DATE: _____   ☐ Sober today

Today's story:

_____

_____

_____

_____

_____

_____

_____

_____

_____

Gifts and challenges:

_____

_____

_____

_____

*In recovery, we never EVER give up on anyone, no matter what it looks
like, no matter how long it takes. Because Grace bats last.
That spiritual WD-40, those water wings, that second wind—it bats last.
That is my promise to you.*

—ANNE LAMOTT

DATE: _____   ☐ Sober today

Today's story:

_____

_____

_____

_____

_____

_____

_____

_____

_____

Gifts and challenges:

_____

_____

_____

_____

Discipline is the bridge between thought and accomplishment.
—JIM ROHN

DATE: _____ ☐ Sober today

Today's story:

_____

_____

_____

_____

_____

_____

_____

_____

Gifts and challenges:

_____

_____

_____

_____

The mind is its own place, and in itself can make a Heav'n of Hell,
and a Hell of Heav'n.
—JOHN MILTON, *PARADISE LOST*

DATE: _____

☐ Sober today

Today's story:

Gifts and challenges:

You don't just choose recovery. You have to keep choosing recovery,
over and over and over again.

—MARYA HORNBACHER

DATE: _____   ☐ Sober today

Today's story:

_____

_____

_____

_____

_____

_____

_____

_____

_____

Gifts and challenges:

_____

_____

_____

_____

You can't go back and make a new start,
but you can start right now and make a brand new ending.
—JAMES R. SHERMAN

DATE: _____   ☐ Sober today

Today's story:

_____

_____

_____

_____

_____

_____

_____

_____

_____

_____

Gifts and challenges:

_____

_____

_____

_____

*If you continue to view the world through a filter created by past events,
then you are allowing your past to control and dictate both
your present and your future.*
—PHILLIP C. MCGRAW

DATE: _____ ☐ Sober today

Today's story:

_____

_____

_____

_____

_____

_____

_____

_____

Gifts and challenges:

_____

_____

_____

_____

Some days, doing "the best we can" may still fall short
of what we would like to be able to do, but life isn't perfect—
on any front—and doing what we can with what we have
is the most we should expect of ourselves or anyone else.
—FRED ROGERS

89

DATE: _____   ☐ Sober today

Today's story:

_____

_____

_____

_____

_____

_____

_____

Gifts and challenges:

_____

_____

_____

The best way out is always through.
—ROBERT FROST

DATE: _____

Today's story:

_____

_____

_____

_____

_____

_____

_____

_____

_____

Gifts and challenges:

_____

_____

_____

_____

You build on failure. You use it as a stepping stone.
Close the door on the past. You don't try to forget the mistakes,
but you don't dwell on it.

—JOHNNY CASH

DATE: _____   ☐ **Sober today**

Today's story:

_____

_____

_____

_____

_____

_____

_____

_____

Gifts and challenges:

_____

_____

_____

Take time at the end of each day to practice gratitude, in which you visualize each object of appreciation while allowing your heart to meet it. Count your blessings.

—BARBARA PAULDING

DATE: _____   ☐ **Sober today**

Today's story:

_____

_____

_____

_____

_____

_____

_____

_____

_____

_____

_____

Gifts and challenges:

_____

_____

_____

_____

Success is the sum of small efforts, repeated day in and day out.
—ROBERT COLLIER

DATE: _____

Today's story:

_____

_____

_____

_____

_____

_____

_____

_____

_____

_____

_____

Gifts and challenges:

_____

_____

_____

Ninety percent of the game is half mental.
—YOGI BERRA

DATE: _____

Today's story:

_____

_____

_____

_____

_____

_____

_____

_____

_____

Gifts and challenges:

_____

_____

_____

_____

*I think you end up doing the stuff you were supposed to do
at the time you were supposed to do it.*

—ROBERT DOWNEY, JR.

DATE: _____   ☐ **Sober today**

Today's story:

_____

_____

_____

_____

_____

_____

_____

_____

_____

_____

Gifts and challenges:

_____

_____

_____

_____

The difference between a stumbling block and a stepping stone
is how high you raise your foot.

—BENNY LEWIS

DATE: _____   ☐ Sober today

Today's story:

....

....

....

....

....

....

....

Gifts and challenges:

....

....

....

....

The trick is in what one emphasizes. We either make ourselves miserable,
or we make ourselves happy. The amount of work is the same.
—CARLOS CASTANEDA

DATE: _____

Today's story:

_____

_____

_____

_____

_____

_____

_____

_____

Gifts and challenges:

_____

_____

_____

_____

Stay afraid, but do it anyway. What's important is the action.
You don't have to wait to be confident. Just do it
and eventually the confidence will follow.

—CARRIE FISHER

DATE: _____   ☐ **Sober today**

Today's story:

_____

_____

_____

_____

_____

_____

_____

Gifts and challenges:

_____

_____

_____

_____

Our greatest glory consists not in never falling,
but in rising every time we fall.

—OLIVER GOLDSMITH

DATE: _____   ☐ Sober today

Today's story:

_____

_____

_____

_____

_____

_____

_____

_____

Gifts and challenges:

_____

_____

_____

_____

Promise me you'll always remember: You're braver than you believe,
and stronger than you seem, and smarter than you think.

—A. A. MILNE, Christopher Robin to Winnie the Pooh

DATE: _____ ☐ Sober today

Today's story:

_____

_____

_____

_____

_____

_____

_____

_____

_____

Gifts and challenges:

_____

_____

_____

_____

*It's our challenges and obstacles that give us layers of depth
and make us interesting. Are they fun when they happen?
No. But they are what make us unique.*

—ELLEN DEGENERES

DATE: _____   ☐ Sober today

Today's story:

_____
_____
_____
_____
_____
_____
_____
_____

Gifts and challenges:

_____
_____
_____
_____

I've been the lead in movies, on television shows and nominated for Emmys.
But the best thing I can say about me is that people who can't stop drinking
come up to me and say, "Can you help me?" And I can say, "Yes."

—MATTHEW PERRY

DATE: _____ ☐ Sober today

Today's story:

_____

_____

_____

_____

_____

_____

_____

_____

_____

Gifts and challenges:

_____

_____

_____

_____

*When you come out of the storm, you won't be the same person
who walked in. That's what this storm's all about.*

—HARUKI MURAKAMI

DATE: _____ ☐ Sober today

Today's story:

_____

_____

_____

_____

_____

_____

_____

_____

_____

Gifts and challenges:

_____

_____

_____

*The most beautiful people we have known are those who have known
defeat, known suffering, known struggle, known loss,
and have found their way out of the depths.*
—ELISABETH KÜBLER-ROSS

DATE: _____   ☐ Sober today

Today's story:

_____

_____

_____

_____

_____

_____

_____

_____

Gifts and challenges:

_____

_____

_____

If you live long enough, you'll make mistakes. But if you learn from them,
you'll be a better person. It's how you handle adversity, not how it affects
you. The main thing is never quit, never quit, never quit.

—WILLIAM J. CLINTON

DATE: _____ ☐ Sober today

Today's story:

_____

_____

_____

_____

_____

_____

_____

_____

Gifts and challenges:

_____

_____

_____

_____

We may encounter many defeats, but we must not be defeated.
—MAYA ANGELOU

DATE: _____   ☐ Sober today

Today's story:

_____

_____

_____

_____

_____

_____

_____

_____

Gifts and challenges:

_____

_____

_____

_____

Your thoughts are the architects of your destiny.
—DAVID O. MCKAY

DATE: _____ ☐ Sober today

Today's story:

_____

_____

_____

_____

_____

_____

_____

_____

_____

_____

Gifts and challenges:

_____

_____

_____

_____

Always concentrate on how far you have come, rather than how far you have left to go. The difference in how easy it seems will amaze you.
—HEIDI JOHNSON

DATE: _____   ☐ Sober today

Today's story:

_____

_____

_____

_____

_____

_____

_____

_____

Gifts and challenges:

_____

_____

_____

_____

To be gritty is to hold fast to an interesting and purposeful goal.
To be gritty is to invest, day after week after year, in challenging practice.
To be gritty is to fall down seven times, and rise eight.

—ANGELA DUCKWORTH

DATE: _____   ☐ Sober today

Today's story:

_____

_____

_____

_____

_____

_____

_____

Gifts and challenges:

_____

_____

_____

_____

*The unfortunate thing about this world is that good habits
are so much easier to give up than bad ones.*

—SOMERSET MAUGHAM

DATE: _____

Today's story:

_____

_____

_____

_____

_____

_____

_____

_____

Gifts and challenges:

_____

_____

_____

_____

*Life is very interesting. ... in the end, some of your greatest pains
become your greatest strengths.*

—DREW BARRYMORE

DATE: _____

Today's story:

_____
_____
_____
_____
_____
_____
_____
_____

Gifts and challenges:

_____
_____
_____
_____

You must learn a new way to think,
before you can master a new way to be.

—MARIANNE WILLIAMSON

112

DATE: _____

Sober today

Today's story:

_____

_____

_____

_____

_____

_____

_____

_____

_____

Gifts and challenges:

_____

_____

_____

_____

Don't let the past steal your present.
—CHERRIE L. MORAGA

DATE: _____   ☐ **Sober today**

Today's story:

_____

_____

_____

_____

_____

_____

_____

_____

_____

Gifts and challenges:

_____

_____

_____

_____

In our daily lives, we must see that it is not happiness that makes us
grateful, but the gratefulness that makes us happy.

—ALBERT CLARKE

DATE: _____   ☐ **Sober today**

Today's story:

_____

_____

_____

_____

_____

_____

_____

_____

_____

Gifts and challenges:

_____

_____

_____

_____

Sometimes we motivate ourselves by thinking of what we want to become.
Sometimes we motivate ourselves by thinking about
who we don't ever want to be again.

—SHANE NIEMEYER

DATE: _____

Sober today

Today's story:

_____

_____

_____

_____

_____

_____

_____

_____

Gifts and challenges:

_____

_____

_____

_____

Life always gives us another chance: It's called "to move on."

—ANA CLAUDIA ANTUNES

DATE: _____   ☐ Sober today

Today's story:

_____

_____

_____

_____

_____

_____

_____

_____

Gifts and challenges:

_____

_____

_____

_____

*Hope begins in the dark, the stubborn hope that if you just show up
and try to do the right thing, the dawn will come.
You wait and watch and work: you don't give up.*

—ANNE LAMOTT

DATE: _____   ☐ Sober today

Today's story:

....

....

....

....

....

....

....

....

....

Gifts and challenges:

....

....

....

....

*People rise out of the ashes, because, at some point, they are invested with
a belief in the possibility of triumph over seemingly impossible odds.*
—ROBERT DOWNEY, JR.

DATE: _____   ☐ Sober today

Today's story:

_____

_____

_____

_____

_____

_____

_____

_____

Gifts and challenges:

_____

_____

_____

_____

You may have to fight a battle more than once to win it.
—MARGARET THATCHER

DATE: _____ ☐ Sober today

Today's story:

_____

_____

_____

_____

_____

_____

_____

_____

_____

Gifts and challenges:

_____

_____

_____

_____

Recovery is not simple abstinence. It's about healing the brain, remembering how to feel, learning how to make good decisions, becoming the kind of person who can engage in healthy relationships, cultivating the willingness to accept help from others, daring to be honest, and opening up to doing.

—DEBRA JAY

DATE: _____ ☐ Sober today

Today's story:

_____

_____

_____

_____

_____

_____

_____

Gifts and challenges:

_____

_____

_____

_____

Never give in, never give in, never, never, never, never—in nothing,
great or small, large or petty—never give in except
to convictions of honor and good sense.
—WINSTON CHURCHILL

DATE: _____   ☐ Sober today

Today's story:

....

....

....

....

....

....

....

....

Gifts and challenges:

....

....

....

Work hard for what you want because it won't come to you without a fight.
—LEAH LABELLE

DATE: _____   ☐ Sober today

Today's story:

_____

_____

_____

_____

_____

_____

_____

Gifts and challenges:

_____

_____

_____

_____

Our life is shaped by our mind; we become what we think.
Joy follows a pure thought like a shadow that never leaves.

—BUDDHA

DATE: _____

Today's story:

_____
_____
_____
_____
_____
_____
_____
_____
_____

Gifts and challenges:

_____
_____
_____

Everything that we do and everyone that we meet
is put in our path for a purpose.
—MARLA GIBBS

DATE: _____

Today's story:

_____

_____

_____

_____

_____

_____

_____

Gifts and challenges:

_____

_____

_____

_____

You simply have to put one foot in front of the other and keep going.
—GEORGE LUCAS

DATE: _____   ☐ Sober today

Today's story:

_____

_____

_____

_____

_____

_____

_____

_____

Gifts and challenges:

_____

_____

_____

_____

Life isn't about waiting for the storm to pass. ...
It's about learning to dance in the rain!

—VIVIAN GREENE

DATE: _____   ☐ Sober today

Today's story:

_____

_____

_____

_____

_____

_____

_____

_____

Gifts and challenges:

_____

_____

_____

_____

The most effective way to do it is to do it.

—AMELIA EARHART

DATE: _____   ☐ **Sober today**

Today's story:

_____

_____

_____

_____

_____

_____

_____

_____

_____

Gifts and challenges:

_____

_____

_____

_____

This above all, to refuse to be a victim.

—MARGARET ATWOOD

DATE: _____   ☐ Sober today

Today's story:

_____

_____

_____

_____

_____

_____

_____

_____

_____

Gifts and challenges:

_____

_____

_____

_____

Human beings are made up of flesh and blood,
and a miracle fiber called courage.

—GEORGE PATTON

DATE: _____   ☐ **Sober today**

Today's story:

_____

_____

_____

_____

_____

_____

_____

_____

_____

_____

Gifts and challenges:

_____

_____

_____

It takes a great deal of courage to stand up to your enemies,
but even more to stand up to your friends.

—J. K. ROWLING

DATE: _____ ☐ Sober today

Today's story:

_____

_____

_____

_____

_____

_____

_____

_____

_____

Gifts and challenges:

_____

_____

_____

_____

You may not control all the events that happen to you,
but you can decide not to be reduced by them.

—MAYA ANGELOU

DATE: _____

Today's story:

_____
_____
_____
_____
_____
_____
_____
_____

Gifts and challenges:

_____
_____
_____
_____

Every morning, when we wake up, we have twenty-four brand-new hours
to live. What a precious gift! We have the capacity to live
in a way that these twenty-four hours will bring peace, joy,
and happiness to ourselves and others.

—THICH NHAT HANH

DATE: _____   ☐ Sober today

Today's story:

_____
_____
_____
_____
_____
_____
_____
_____

Gifts and challenges:

_____
_____
_____

Many people have a wrong idea of what constitutes true happiness.
It is not attained through self-gratification but through
fidelity to a worthy purpose.
—HELEN KELLER

DATE: _____ ☐ Sober today

Today's story:

_____

_____

_____

_____

_____

_____

_____

_____

Gifts and challenges:

_____

_____

_____

_____

Anyone can be a star, anyone can be a champion in their own life:
that is the real truth for you to claim and live.
—PHILLIP C. MCGRAW

DATE: _____

Today's story:

_____

_____

_____

_____

_____

_____

_____

_____

_____

Gifts and challenges:

_____

_____

_____

_____

Be patient towards all that is unsolved in your heart,
and learn to love the questions themselves.
—RAINER MARIA RILKE

DATE: _____   ☐ **Sober today**

Today's story:

_____

_____

_____

_____

_____

_____

_____

_____

Gifts and challenges:

_____

_____

_____

_____

It is never too late to be what you might have been.
—GEORGE ELIOT

DATE: _____   ☐ Sober today

Today's story:

_____

_____

_____

_____

_____

_____

_____

Gifts and challenges:

_____

_____

_____

_____

Life loves to be taken by the lapel and be told:
"I am with you kid. Let's go."
—MAYA ANGELOU

DATE: _____ ☐ Sober today

Today's story:

_____

_____

_____

_____

_____

_____

_____

Gifts and challenges:

_____

_____

_____

Everything we do in life is based on agreements we have made—
agreements with ourselves, with other people, with society, with God.
But the most important agreements are the ones we make with ourselves.
—DON MIGUEL RUIZ, *THE FOUR AGREEMENTS*

DATE: _____ ☐ Sober today

Today's story:

_____

_____

_____

_____

_____

_____

_____

_____

_____

Gifts and challenges:

_____

_____

_____

_____

You're imperfect, and you're wired for struggle,
but you are worthy of love and belonging.
—BRENÉ BROWN

DATE: _____   ☐ Sober today

Today's story:

_____

_____

_____

_____

_____

_____

_____

_____

_____

_____

Gifts and challenges:

_____

_____

_____

Recovery is hard. Regret is harder.
—BRITTANY BURGUNDER

DATE: _____ ☐ Sober today

Today's story:

_____

_____

_____

_____

_____

_____

_____

_____

Gifts and challenges:

_____

_____

_____

_____

Life doesn't get easier or more forgiving, we get stronger and more resilient.
—STEVE MARABOLI

DATE: _____   ☐ Sober today

Today's story:

_____

_____

_____

_____

_____

_____

_____

_____

Gifts and challenges:

_____

_____

_____

Pain in this life is not avoidable, but the pain
we create avoiding pain is avoidable.

—R. D. LAING

142

DATE: _____   ☐ Sober today

Today's story:

_____

_____

_____

_____

_____

_____

_____

_____

Gifts and challenges:

_____

_____

_____

_____

Believe you can and you're halfway there.
—THEODORE ROOSEVELT

DATE: _____   ☐ Sober today

Today's story:

_____

_____

_____

_____

_____

_____

_____

_____

Gifts and challenges:

_____

_____

_____

_____

There is no such thing as a lack of faith. We all have plenty of faith, it's just that we have faith in the wrong things. We have faith in what can't be done rather than what can be done. … Faith is a law.

—ERIC BUTTERWORTH

DATE: _____

☐ **Sober today**

Today's story:

_____

_____

_____

_____

_____

_____

_____

_____

Gifts and challenges:

_____

_____

_____

_____

Courage is being scared to death, but saddling up anyway.
—JOHN WAYNE

DATE: _____ ☐ Sober today

Today's story:

_____
_____
_____
_____
_____
_____
_____
_____

Gifts and challenges:

_____
_____
_____
_____

As human beings, our greatness lies not so much in being able to remake the world ... as in being able to remake ourselves.

—MAHATMA GANDHI

DATE: _____

☐ Sober today

Today's story:

_____
_____
_____
_____
_____
_____
_____
_____
_____

Gifts and challenges:

_____
_____
_____
_____

Life shrinks or expands in proportion to one's courage.
—ANAÏS NIN

DATE: _____ ☐ Sober today

Today's story:

_____

_____

_____

_____

_____

_____

_____

_____

_____

_____

Gifts and challenges:

_____

_____

_____

_____

Whether you think that you can or that you can't, you are usually right.
—HENRY FORD

DATE: _____   ☐ Sober today

Today's story:

_____

_____

_____

_____

_____

_____

_____

_____

Gifts and challenges:

_____

_____

_____

_____

Always bear in mind that your own resolution to success
is more important than any other one thing.
—ABRAHAM LINCOLN

DATE: _____   ☐ Sober today

Today's story:

_____

_____

_____

_____

_____

_____

_____

_____

Gifts and challenges:

_____

_____

_____

Everything can be taken from a man but one thing:
the last of human freedoms—to choose one's attitude in any
given set of circumstances, to choose one's own way.

—VIKTOR FRANKL

DATE: _____ ☐ Sober today

Today's story:

_____

_____

_____

_____

_____

_____

_____

_____

_____

_____

_____

_____

Gifts and challenges:

_____

_____

_____

_____

Hardships often prepare ordinary people for an extraordinary destiny.
—C. S. LEWIS

DATE: _____ ☐ **Sober today**

Today's story:

_____

_____

_____

_____

_____

_____

_____

Gifts and challenges:

_____

_____

_____

_____

Healing is a matter of time, but it is sometimes also
a matter of opportunity.
—HIPPOCRATES

DATE: _____

☐ Sober today

Today's story:

_____
_____
_____
_____
_____
_____
_____

Gifts and challenges:

_____
_____
_____

There is a crack in everything. That's how the light gets in.
—LEONARD COHEN

DATE: _____   ☐ Sober today

Today's story:

_____

_____

_____

_____

_____

_____

_____

_____

Gifts and challenges:

_____

_____

_____

_____

Some of us think holding on makes us strong, but sometimes it is letting go.
—HERMAN HESSE

DATE: _____   ☐ Sober today

Today's story:

_____

_____

_____

_____

_____

_____

_____

_____

_____

_____

Gifts and challenges:

_____

_____

_____

_____

You take your life in your own hands, and what happens?
A terrible thing: no one to blame.
—ERICA JONG

THE ROAD AHEAD

Your life will be a great and continuous unfolding.
—CHERYL STRAYED

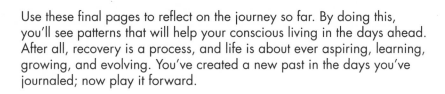

Use these final pages to reflect on the journey so far. By doing this, you'll see patterns that will help your conscious living in the days ahead. After all, recovery is a process, and life is about ever aspiring, learning, growing, and evolving. You've created a new past in the days you've journaled; now play it forward.

Where are you now compared to where you were when you started this journal? Where will you go from here?

What are you proudest of? Most grateful for?

Knowing what you know now since beginning this journal, what advice would you give yourself for the road ahead?

You can't go back and make a new start, but you can start right now and make a brand new ending.

—JAMES R. SHERMAN